Jack Ma:
A Lesson in Trust, Honor, and Shared Prosperity

Jack Ma:
A Lesson in Trust, Honor, and Shared Prosperity

Reinventing the Motivations of Commerce - Insight and Analysis into the Life of Asia's Richest Man

JR MacGregor

Jack Ma: A Lesson in Trust, Honor, and Shared Prosperity

Reinventing the Motivations of Commerce – Insight and Analysis into the Life of Asia's Richest Man

Copyright © 2018 JR MacGregor

All rights reserved. No portion of this book may be reproduced, stored in a retrieval system, or transmitted in any form or by any means – electronic, mechanical, photocopy, recording, scanning, or other – except for brief quotations in critical reviews or articles, without prior written permission of the publisher.

Published by CAC Publishing LLC.

ISBN 978-1-948489-90-4 paperback

ISBN 978-1-948489-89-8 eBook

This book is dedicated to those who study great men in hopes of one day joining their ranks. Remember, studying and finding what works is only half the battle, it's up to you to implement what you learn and take massive action, so that, one day, you may be studied yourself.

Contents

Foreword 10

Introduction 15

Chapter 1 Jack 20

Chapter 2 Academic Life 22

Chapter 3 The Internet 25

Chapter 4 Question Everything........................ 30

Chapter 5 Championing Shared Prosperity 35

Chapter 6 His Own Man 40

Chapter 7 Choices 45

Chapter 8 Understand Your Motivation 50

Chapter 9 Jack's Four Failures............................ 56

Chapter 10 See the Big Picture 61

Chapter 11 Saving 66

Chapter 12 Infinite Game.................................... 71

Conclusion 77

Foreword

What is it about men who scale great heights and reach the summit? Why are we enticed by such success? Why do we yearn to know their secret sauce?

I think it is because we are looking for the spark that will ignite our own giant within. I think it is because we know deep down that we are meant for greatness and achievement, but we are at a loss as to how to go about getting it.

It turns out that the best way for us to find our own spark is to observe the way others have found theirs, but, because no two people get their spark in an identical fashion, we can't find all the pieces to our own puzzle in one place. Instinctively, we have a curiosity that becomes insatiable until we find our own groove.

During my own pursuit to understand success and achievement, I have found a number of recurring themes that apply regardless of what stage of my life I happen to be at. There are three of these truths.

The first, most relevant, truth presents itself as an irony. It is the fact that we are all different, yet we are all the same. Each of us has more dimensions than our one-track mind can initially fathom. The reason so many of the things that work seem so bizarre and nonsensical is that we are all different yet the same. There are areas of our life that can seem completely different on the surface, but on closer inspection we find more similarity than difference.

The second truth is that we typically repel those who are most like us. If you find that you hate something in a person, the chances are very high that you actually have something in common with them. You can use this to your benefit. Observe and take note of the feelings you have about someone, but refrain from criticism. Keep criticism to a minimum, or to none at all, because today's criticism becomes tomorrow's barrier to advancement. In your pursuit of success, everyone has something to contribute.

The third and final truth is that success is not just about mastering one single aspect of action. It is not about having great vision like Jack Ma when he, in the early days, recognized what the internet could represent. It is not just about the attention to detail that Steve Jobs showed us. It is not just about empathy like Elon Musk and Richard Branson display.

Each individual ingredient is complex in depth and shade, with more complexity than the words used to describe them can convey. To be successful, we need to have each these single filaments of success and weave them together to form our own cloak of invincibility. Since no word can capture the true meaning of each individual characteristic needed to be successful, we are left to the next best thing, and that is to personify these individual characteristics of success in men who have come to embody them.

It helps that our species is a curious bunch and we want knowledge—we want to know what it is, how to make, and how to use it. Likewise, when it comes to success, we want to know what its characteristics are, how to emulate those characteristics, and how to apply that knowledge to our own corner of the world. And, so, we want to know how successful men become successful.

On our path to develop our own personal suite of characteristics, we constantly try new things to see how they fit. It is like trying on a new shoe. We try it, see if it fits. If it suits us, and if it works, we hang on to it. If it does not, we put it back, and try something else. That is, in essence, what making mistakes and experiencing failure is all about. It is improbable that every new thing you try is going to work every time. It is good to be curious about everything.

Studying Jack Ma provides a wealth of material for understanding the human condition and spirit. Unlike the many other accomplished men I have studied, Ma was raised in a very different culture. Jack Ma is a beacon embodying pure intention and desire winning against forces of circumstance. His story demonstrates that it is possible to make something out of nothing, and to advance positively through a sea of negativity. Culture, geolocation, initial surroundings, and circumstances have only a small part to play in how one's life unfolds.

If there is such a thing as fate, it is not determined by where you are born. That is liberating to understand, wherever you come from. So often, in today's world, we are brought face to face with the diversity of our origins. Forces to exclude those of diverse origins try to rise against the voices that champion the desire to include. While I can understand the fear of displacement, I find inclusion to be a wholly better endeavor, something that Jack Ma exemplifies.

I hope you find as much insight from this book as I did while writing it. I hope you come closer to your own truth and find your own wings to fly. May success be your guide and achievement your goal.

***

Introduction

"The very important thing you should have is patience."

Jack Ma

Hangzhou is a city located southwest of Shanghai. It sits by Hangzhou Bay which connects to the East China Sea. It is a vibrant city in today's China, dominated by commerce and industry. Today, the mention of China evokes images of large factories and vibrant commerce, large populations, and delectable food. It was not so in 1965. 1965's China was a very different story, and Hangzhou a very different place.

Jack Ma, China's richest man until recently, was born in Hangzhou, on October 15, 1965, to working parents and a modest lifestyle. He was born Ma Yun, the middle of the three siblings, with an older brother and younger sister. He was seven years old before he realized there was a world beyond the land speaking his native tongue.

Richard Nixon had entered the White House and begun to make strides in opening a path to Beijing. In 1972, Nixon's historical trip to Beijing included a visit to Hangzhou, which put the town on the map and marked it as a destination for throngs of tourists. With Nixon's arrival, Ma learned that a whole new world existed somewhere out there, and his mind was lit. That new revelation combined with the opportunity to meet people from the new world redrew Ma's path and changed the trajectory of his life.

By any measure, Jack Ma was an average kid. There was nothing spectacular or outstanding about this scrawny kid. He was small for his age, and that attracted the bullies like bees to honey. The way he responded to being picked on constantly at school shaped the way he has behaved the rest of his life. Ma found a part of himself that could stand up to bullies. Like all of us presented with adversity, we face choices. We can choose to run or fight. When young Jack was faced with this choice, he stood his ground and fought. At first, there was not a lot of winning. He did get knocked around a bit, but he learned, and he fought back, not because he was the belligerent sort, but because he was staking his claim to the spot where he was standing.

Being the scrawny kid can be a challenging affair. You need to be twice as brave to make up for your slight presence, and you have to be fast. Jack was naturally fast—both in agility and in thinking. This helped get him out of trouble and ahead of the game even as a kid.

Jack Ma spent much of his childhood entertaining himself in a city that was fairly cultural and ethnic. Remember, China in the sixties was changing in a staggering way. Infrastructure change was accompanied by changes in outlook, fashion, values, and lifestyle. Back then, rising to the top of the pile was a lot more difficult, especially if you are not one connected to the corridors of power. To make it in China as an outsider was unheard off. And Jack Ma was the quintessential outsider, as you will see through the unfolding of his life.

Ma was a typical kid, curious about everything, from language to crickets. He was also observant. One of his favorite hobbies was collecting crickets on the outskirts of Hangzhou and pitting them in battles against each other. He went to great lengths to understand those crickets so that he'd have the best ones he could find and would be able to win the next matchup. He became so good at it that he could identify the best crickets with great accuracy simply by listening to the sounds they made. He could pick the winners just by watching them for a few minutes.

Later, in a speech, Jack Ma was to say, *"The very important thing you should have is patience."* The patience Ma describes is not about letting the chips fall where they may, but is a very deliberate and powerful sort of patience, uncommon among successful men. It is the patience of the waters of the Colorado River imperceptibly chiseling through the rock to form the Grand Canyon.

Throughout his life, Jack Ma's work has been a blend of hurry and patience. It has been like powerfully and relentlessly turning the wheel of a grinding stone but giving the stone the time it needs to sharpen the blade, rather than stopping it every few minutes to see if the work is done. This is the same kind of patience the Stoics were about.

There are three direct consequences of developing patience. The first is that you get to enter the nature of things and understand your actions in a way that is deep and thorough. This allows you to go further than others would, and that, in turn, allows you to succeed when others fail.

The second consequence of developing patience is that it staves off frustration and allows you to do what is necessary when it is called for, without wasting mental and physical resources by worrying and fretting over outcomes.

Third, having patience allows the universe to do its part. You can only do half the work when you want to bake a cake. After the batter is done, you need to let the oven do its thing. If you keep opening the oven door and letting the air out, you are going to have a poorly baked cake. When I compare myself to Jack Ma, I realize that patience is something I could have used a lot more of in my life. Do you have enough patience?

***

Chapter 1 Jack

"People think, 'Jack, you do too much'."

Jack Ma

It was 1972 and Richard Nixon had just made his historic visit to China to normalize Sino-US relations. While he was there, Nixon met with Mao Zedong and Zhou Enlai, visiting three cities, Beijing, Shanghai, and Jack Ma's birthplace of Hangzhou. That visit had a direct impact on six year old Ma Yun.

With the thawing Sino-American relationships, tourists and businesses from the United States flocked to the newly opened China. One of the places they flocked to was Hangzhou. The tourism industry was one of the first areas of commerce to see a boom in the wake of Nixon's efforts. The little, free-spirited Ma Yun was exposed to an entirely new culture from across the waters of the East China Sea while the hotel and tourism industry started to boom in Hangzhou.

In his teenage years, Ma Yun's fascination with the new cultures and new languages prompted him to learn English, but, since he could not afford to take English lessons and they weren't taught in school, he decided to do the next best thing. He began to barter for it. In return for tours of the city, he would ask American tourists to teach him how to speak English. It was an effective and creative way to learn English.

As Ma Yun spent time with the tourists, showing them around town and learning their language, he realized that life did not have to be limited to the way the Chinese did things, or to the way the Ma household did things. He realized that the world out there was large, larger than what he could possibly imagine, and he was determined to make something of it.

He gained one more thing from his endeavors that remains with him to this day. Aside from learning English from these tourists, he also acquired the name Jack. So, one day out of the blue, he left home as Ma Yun, and came back as Jack Ma.

***

Chapter 2 Academic Life

"China is still the fastest growing economy in the world, but we need to learn how to use money in a better way, and it's about quality, not quantity."

Jack Ma

We are often fooled into thinking that, without the proper educational background or name-brand college certificate, we are destined to follow a less desirable path, but that is not always the case, especially today. However, like many before, Jack Ma decided that the first thing he needed to do if he wanted to get ahead was get an education.

The educational system in China is not as liberal as in the United States; you cannot just walk into a school, and say, "Here I am." In China, you must sit for rigorous tests at the National level, and your scores determine which college or university you can go to. The tests are not optional like the SATs or the APs in the USA. In China, if you take the tests and fail, you are not going anywhere. And Jack failed twice.

Taking standardized tests in China is nothing like taking the college entrance exams in the USA. The Chinese tests are tough. If I were to bet, I would wager that more than two-thirds of US college graduates wouldn't be able to get through China's college entrance exams. They are designed to be tough and separate the wheat from the chaff.

Sometimes you don't get what you want on the first couple of tries. When Ma went back for the third time, he was better prepared. He had resolved to do whatever he needed to, and he hit the books hard. Jack Ma passed the exams and was able to attend teacher's college, eventually graduating as an English teacher. His barters from two decades before had paid off—but not as much as they eventually would.

Jack Ma was an average student, not because he was lazy or slow on the pick-up, but because he was focused on different things than the typical student. He was diligent, no doubt, but his heart was elsewhere. He knew there was more to life than he could get from sitting in a one-size-fits-all classroom.

Yet, while Ma was all about celebrating his own unique perspective and his unique pursuits, he also knew one thing we all need to realize sometime in our lives. Even successful men like Andrew Carnegie and

Jeff Bezos have known that we all need to do what is necessary for today's living while we prepare for tomorrow's success. So, when Jack Ma graduated teacher's training college, he taught English for $12 a month.

***

Chapter 3 The Internet

"I know nothing about technology."

Jack Ma

We live in a unique time with a new phenomenon called the internet. For the first time ever, we now have an adult population that has known the internet since their birth. The Millennials, as this cohort is called, is the generation born between the 80s and the mid-90s. This generation has always been fully immersed in the internet.

The older Generation X crowd occupies another unique position, starting life when there was still no internet, watching its birth, and seeing, with amazement, how far the internet has come during their lifetime. That is the generation of Jack Ma.

When he first saw the internet up close, Jack Ma was electrified, with the same instincts emerging as he felt when he saw the first batch of foreigners in Hangzhou as a kid. The internet fueled some of his wildest imaginings, and he instinctively knew that an opportunity like no other right was before his eyes.

When we see the internet as a normal state of daily life and events, we can become blind to it in a way that Jack Ma was not. We see the internet as a source of goods, services, content, and connection. Jack saw the internet as an open portal to reach out the world. Even though he had no coding or programming experience, he knew the internet was a frontier he needed to explore.

Jack Ma still knows nothing about technology other than what he absorbs through the daily operation of his company. But therein lies the essence of what it means to be successful. You do not need to know the nuts and bolts of something to make it big. You do not need to be an inventor to make it big. We don't all need to be a Thomas Edison or an Alexander Graham Bell. Henry Ford did not need to redesign the wheel to multiply the market for automobiles. Steve Jobs did not need to know how to solder a motherboard, and Richard Branson did not need to know how to read a balance sheet. Yet, each one understood the value they could contribute to the value chain.

Jack Ma today still does not know how to code, but he knows how to create value in a global trading and payment system that is one of the largest in the world. When Alibaba debuted on the NYSE, it was the largest IPO the market had ever seen—$168 billion.

When they ended their first day of trading on the NYSE, Jack Ma said, "What we raised today is not money, it is trust." That statement reveals that Jack Ma sees Alibaba as an extension of himself, one that is part of the value he offers the world, and that the value he offers is the trust of the participants in the market he created.

There is no success to be had unless it is based on value. Your contribution is not complete until you add that value. Success is when your contribution adds so much value for others that the only way they can pay you for it is by rewarding you. But that reward isn't what you go after in your pursuit of success—you go after achieving a level of contribution that no one else can offer.

Jack Ma saw the opportunity to add value to a marketplace that was missing one essential component. There was a problem with trust in the online marketplace. What Ma brought to that market was the ability to instill confidence in the buyer. When he earned that trust, he was able to catapult the company to stratospheric heights. On Singles Day, China's answer to Valentines Day, Alibaba had a sale that totaled more than $18 billion in sales. That would not have been possible were it not for the trust that Ma had structured into every transaction made through Alibaba.

Jack Ma's contribution was to touch buyers and sellers alike and reach out to them across vast seas and across borders. Ma's version of success has been based on trust and structuring that trust into every transaction. Have you ever tried to buy anything from Alibaba? They have options to choose shipping with or without tracking numbers. Whenever I place an order, I take free shipping without the tracking number, and, yet, not once in the many times I have made a purchase have I not received what I ordered. Think about that for a minute. How do you institutionalize that sort of efficiency and trust?

That was the value Jack Ma created and executed; trust was the lynchpin in creating a robust and efficient market. It isn't just the seller who has benefited, it is the buyer as well. Buyers go on to add their own value, reselling their products to other customers. Without Alibaba and Alipay, there would be a huge hit to global trade—and to the capacity for wealth creation that has been made available to the smaller guy.

The day Alibaba hit a market share of $168 billion was a testament to the trust Jack Ma has been passionate about creating in the marketplace. It was the value that he added—and he was rewarded with a $25 billion personal payday.

***

Chapter 4 Question Everything

"Before I left China, I was educated that China was the richest, happiest country in the world. So, when I arrived in Australia, I thought, 'Oh my God, everything is different from what I was told.' Since then, I started to think differently."

Jack Ma

As a kid growing up, whether in China or just about anywhere else, you are not aware of the politics and take for granted the biases. All you may hear is that you are from the best country—until you actually meet someone from another country.

It wasn't until Jack Ma got outside China and began to travel the world that he realized that there is a difference between the hype and the reality. He realized that many conventional truths weren't really truths at all, and that, if he wanted to get the real story, he needed to question everything.

In 1995, Ma traveled to the United States on behalf of a client who was looking for a solution to an accounts receivable issue. At the time, Jack had an English-Chinese translation business, often helping clients with more than translation. During that trip, Jack Ma was introduced to the internet and shown how to find anything using a search engine. To his dismay, when he tried to find Chinese beer, his search came up empty. He wasn't even able to find any Chinese websites on the internet, so he decided to do something about that.

When he got back to China, he set up an internet company focused on building websites for Chinese businesses. (This was not Alibaba yet.) Ma was interested in accomplishing three things. First, he wanted to create a platform for his countrymen to get out onto the world stage. Second, he wanted the rest of the world to know China, how far it had come, and what it had to offer. Finally, he wanted to take advantage of the opportunity that he saw so plainly.

So, Jack Ma set up China Pages. At its heart, China Pages was a cross border effort in international trade, introducing the new China to the rest of the world. That was 1995, and China had been building up its capacity for some time and was well on its way to becoming a manufacturing powerhouse. This large industrial complex had created numerous small and medium enterprises (SMEs) that were open to international business but didn't yet know or understand how to get that international business. Ma's idea was to give them a leg up on the international scene by having China Pages act as a portal into China.

To expand the scope of the business, Ma teamed up with a few friends, and brought in a government entity as a partner. The idea was to expand China Pages with an infusion of resources and to have the government agency open doors in the right places. It did not turn out as he had planned. Instead, Ma found the bureaucracy stifling. There wasn't much Jack Ma could do, so rather than fighting an uphill battle, he quit and moved on.

Ma went on to get a job at the Ministry of Foreign Trade and Economic Cooperation. This wasn't what he really wanted to do, but the opportunity proved beneficial in the long run. He made strong connections through the job, one of which was with Jerry Yang, the founder of Yahoo.

Upon leaving the ministry a short time later, Jack Ma spent some time soul searching. He had an inner drive, and a lot of built-up frustration and pent up energy. Even now, anyone who meets him instantly recognizes the wound-up energy that pervades his presence. It is not frustration or anger—it is simply unbridled energy that comes from battling with whatever hand life deals you. It is the same energy that kept him going as he got rejected time and again, for everything from a job at KFC to admissions at Harvard. (At KFC he was the only person to be rejected out of 24 applicants. He applied to Harvard and was rejected ten times.)

That kind of raw energy is not sustainable without a purpose and vision to direct it. Jack was intent on going somewhere. He may have not consciously been aware of where that might be, but he discovered the direction that would consume him when he was at the keys of a computer in the United States, unable to find a single Chinese company when he searched for Chinese beer.

Jack Ma has moved from nationalistic motivations to altruistic motivations over the years as he increasingly sees the whole world as a common humanity, not as geography with political lines drawn across them. His original idea of the need for jobs for all Chinese has grown into the desire to spread jobs and prosperity to all people regardless of their street address.

Ma has said that SMEs are the instruments of wealth creation, and he wants to see every SME become larger than Amazon. He sees himself as the enabler that would facilitate this revolution. He has looked into the future, saying,

> *"Every revolution takes about fifty years."*
>
> Jack Ma

Chapter 5 Championing Shared Prosperity

"As a business person, I want the world to share the prosperity together."

Jack Ma

Jack Ma is motivated by many of the same things that typical Fortune 500 companies are, but one thing that is front and center in his mind, which rarely occurs to the others, is shared prosperity, or prosperity for all.

Ma wants to raise China and its millions of workers to a level of prosperity yet unseen in that country. But his desire to elevate the man on the street does not stop at China's borders but reaches around the world. That was one reason he recently pledged to the American President that he would create a million jobs in the United States.

Ma believes that shared prosperity comes from shared contribution. That means that everyone must have a job; everyone needs to be employed and contributing to each other's success, thereby creating a shared success and shared prosperity.

For Jack Ma, this starts at the local level. The idea behind Alibaba, and China Pages, was to advance businesses in China and launch them onto the world stage. But it doesn't stop there.

Ma understands acutely that one's prosperity is dependent upon another's. He sees global trade as crucial to joint prosperity. Ma's vision is motivated by more than money. Ma has brought his vision of pulling together the four corners of the world to the global stage. He sees that as inextricably linked to global free trade, and so he has been unhappy with the possibility of restrictive trade policies.

The key success factor necessary to institute Jack Ma's philosophy is trust. For him, trust is the foundation that needs to underpin all of his businesses and is at the heart of all that connects the world.

In 2011, an event was to test Jack Ma's core value of trust. Ma was devastated when it came to light that outright fraud taking place within Alibaba. It struck at the core of Jack's empire. A number of employees were found to have been awarding Gold Star status to undeserving vendors. It was not an innocent error, or someone not doing their job properly. It was outright fraud with the intent to cheat Alibaba's customers.

Alibaba awarded Gold Star status to vendors who had proven themselves repeatedly. When they were awarded this rating, it gave buyers on Alibaba a sense of trust in the vendor and its products. This was one of the ways Alibaba bridged the trust gap in the electronic marketplace. It was an obvious and important part of their reputation management system.

Unfortunately, some unscrupulous employees had colluded with outsiders to set up shops selling all kinds of electronic goods. There were more than a couple of hundred involved, taking orders and payments—but not delivering the products.

When the fraud was exposed, the always smiling, pint-sized Jack, flew into rage, because the scam had attacked one of the most important things he had worked so hard to build and maintain—trust. He had taken many steps to institutionalize trust and this act would diminish that. The frauds threatened a lot more than the affected customers. It threatened Jack's vision of shared prosperity.

Jack Ma had brought a firm belief in a set of principles into the culture of Alibaba and into all the companies he created. As a persona and head of the company,

Ma directed the company to adhere to a specific priority of allegiance. His principles were to always champion the customer first, the employee second, and the investor third. Many times prior to the IPO, and even during the IPO, Ma said,

> *"If you want to invest in us, we believe customer No. 1, employee No. 2, shareholder No. 3. If they do not want to buy that, that is fine. If they regret, they can sell us."*

That has been his mantra. He firmly believes that each company stands only because of the customer, and that he can only realize the goal of large scale employment for the masses if the customer patronizes his company. Without the customer, everything else falls apart.

Imagine, if you can, what it must have felt like for a man with such priorities and convictions to discover that the second most important group on his list of priorities was actively betraying the first, and, in so doing, were corrupting his values and jeopardizing his dream of mass employment. That event was the beginning of one of the hardest times in Jack Ma's life.

Ma could have taken the easy way out and swept it under the rug. Instead, he fired more than a hundred people who were directly or indirectly involved in the fraud. He even fired the CEO and the COO, because upper management is ultimately responsible for all that goes on. In the end, there was about $2 million worth of losses that he had to take responsibility for. It was a simple decision for him. Not doing so would have let down the group Ma regards as the lynchpin of shared prosperity.

Whether you call this ethics or morals doesn't matter, but these principles are lacking in much of the business world today. Many business leaders have become so myopic they have forgotten that the customer is the key to their survival.

***

Chapter 6 His Own Man

"When I am myself, I am happy and have a good result."

Jack Ma

Everyone who knew Jack Ma before his rise to fame and fortune describes him as being completely ordinary. His wife even goes one step further, and says that Ma is not the best-looking person in the world, but she was more interested in him for the way he thought and his tenacity for getting things done.

From looks to personality, from demeanor to gait, from intellect to talent, Jack Ma was in many ways unremarkable. But Zhang Ying also saw that this young man of 5'3" at teacher's college was different in his outlook and spark. What he lacked in height, looks, or presence, he made up for in spades with tenacity, energy, and ideas. Jack Ma and Zhang Ying were married right after college and stitched together a living on a teacher's salary of $12 a month.

No one, even Zhang Ying, ever thought that Jack Mas was anyone other than he seemed to be or that he was pretending to be something that he was not. There was no air of duplicity about him, nor any air of arrogance about anything that he undertook. Jack Ma has no illusions about who he is. You know how some people think they are all that when they have nothing to show for it? Jack Ma, even today, has none of that.

What Jack Ma was always true to were his own stars. He worked hard, he had ostentatious dreams, and he pulled out all the stops to make it happen.

Zhang was shocked and worried at the same time, but she went along with it when, one day, out of the blue, Jack resigned from his teaching position and announced to her that he wanted to begin his own business. This was years before their Alibaba days. On the surface, there was not one leg to stand on for this decision, but she had always felt instinctively that there was more to Jack than his physical attributes would suggest.

She was constantly unsettled as day after day went by, and Jack Ma's first business floundered. The business, Haibo Translation Agency, provided English translation services to locals. They made about $30 a month, but rent alone was about $95., so there was always a shortfall in revenue. To make up the difference and pay the bills at the translation business, Jack would go to the market at Yiwu in

Guangzhou, and sell odds and ends to shoppers. It took three years, but Ma finally managed to make the translation business a success.

Just as Zhang Ying began to breathe a sigh of relief, Jack turned the tables on her again by starting China Pages. Then, he took another leap to start his ecommerce venture. Zhang Ying's growing worry and stress only increased when Jack announced that he planned to borrow 500,000 Yuan to start the website for it.

Soon, Jack Ma had put together a group of sixteen people and persuaded them to put their money in, but he gave them fair warning. He told them that they could either lose it all, or they could become richer than anything they could imagine. His investors included friends, colleagues, and students.

Jack brought Zhang Ying into the picture and told her he wanted her to be his general—his right-hand person—but for that, she had to quit her job and relinquish the only stable source of income in the family. According to Jack, the reason for having his wife quit her job and come on board Alibaba was to make everyone else feel safe that the endeavor was an all-in effort by the family and not some idle hair-brained scheme. Jack Ma was consumed by the importance of trust and the perception of it. Like Gandhi, Ma knew from a young age that being truthful alone was not enough, that it was equally important, if not more so, to be perceived as such.

With 16 people and his wife, with one son on the way, Alibaba was born. In its early stages, Alibaba sucked up a lot of the oxygen in the Ma home for Jack and the others who came there. The Ma home was the central office for all brainstorming and working ideas. They worked day in and day out. If the others were not there and Jack Ma had an inspiration, they would all be there and hard at work on the idea in 10 minutes.

As much as Zhang Ying was originally supposed to be a key member of the founding team, her duties as hostess became prioritized. As a member of a Chinese household, it was up to the mistress of the home to host and take care of all those who visited. Whatever their financial situation was, meals and refreshments needed to be provided as a matter of courtesy, and Zhang Ying executed that responsibility gracefully.

Times were tight. All the founding members took 500 Yuan from the company to sustain themselves. In the Ma household, that was used as part of the budget for feeding their guests when they were there.

This went on for more than a year. Toil, sweat, smoke, and long days rolled into longer nights. At the end of the year, when Zhang Ying asked him how much they made, Jack did not have much to report. It was a devastating conversation for both. But Jack punctuated that terse conversation with a prediction that one day they would make income enough to pay one million in taxes per day.

***

Chapter 7 Choices

"When we first started our internet company, 'China Pages,' in 1995, and we were just making home pages for a lot of Chinese companies. We went to the big owners, the big companies, and they did not want to do it. We go to state-owned companies, and they did not want to do it. Only the small and medium companies really want to do it."

Jack Ma

Sweat and toil weren't the only price Jack and Zhang Ying paid for their success at Alibaba. Beyond the usual sacrifices, there was one significant price the Mas were about to pay, and they did not know it at the time. Their son, who was born the same year Alibaba was founded, had been left to grow up virtually alone while the adults around him, from the Mas to all the founders and workers who hung out at the Ma household, worked.

The company got the lion's share of the parents' attention. Their son grew up in the same smoke-filled room as the rest of the people working on Alibaba. Young Ma was a product of that environment.

Without sufficient parental guidance from his parents, young Ma began to develop in an unwanted direction. Unsurprisingly, young Ma, having grown up surrounded by talk of the internet, ended up spending time in internet bars and online gaming centers at a young age as soon as he was given a little freedom. That is not typically a great way to spend one's youth.

At just ten years of age, the young Ma was having problems at school and was excessively disobedient with his parents. His teachers were not happy with his academics and his social skills. The causes of young Ma's problems were finally identified as the lack of parental guidance and the loneliness he experienced from spending so much time without his parents' attention. When Zhang Ying reported these developments to Jack, Jack was in shock. They had both missed the writing on the wall. All of their success at Alibaba had been at the cost of their son's emotional and psychological development.

The Mas made a two-pronged assault on the problem.

First, Jack Ma took an unconventional approach to the problem. Jack gave his son 200 Yuan and told him to go play online games with his friends. He gave the boy permission to spend all of it and stay out for as long as he wanted. He was gone for three days. When he returned, he was hungry and exhausted, so he was fed well and put to bed. When he woke up, Jack was waiting for him, and they had a simple conversation. Jack asked his son what he had gained from all those internet games. He asked him where the money went. What had he gained from it? The approach was unusual, but it had the intended effect. It got the young Ma to wake up and recognize the outcome of his choices.

Second, Zhang Ying began to stay home to look after him. Zhang Ying stepped back from her responsibilities at Alibaba, which had, by this point, grown and was doing very well. At home, Zhang Ying stayed with their son every minute of the day. Within a short period of time, it was enough to turn the boy around, and both his grades and social demeanor started to improve.

That event had an impact on the Ma household. Internet games became a taboo subject at home. Even when Jack Ma had the opportunity to invest in them, he stayed away. It was not something he wanted to be a part of.

We all make choices and decisions. Every action is the result of a choice. Sometimes those choices have unforeseen consequences. In economics, we typically call this the *opportunity cost*. It exists for all actions.

All actions have an alternative, whether you see it or not. Everything you do is a choice; everything you do has an alternative. Even sitting down and doing nothing is an alternative.

However, you cannot dwell in regret or stop taking action because the alternative you may not see or think of was actually the better choice. You need to keep moving forward. The only way you can reconcile with your choices is by not practicing the indiscipline of regret. Those who know that everything is a choice also know that once they have made their choice, there can be no regret. If you play the regret game, every choice you make will never be good enough, and your thoughts can stray to the alternative you didn't choose and the benefits that could have flowed from it.

Look at it in another way. When Jack had the opportunity to start Alibaba and his son was born at the same time, Jack Ma had a choice. What if he had decided to focus on raising his son, instead of diving into Alibaba? Certainly, Jack's son would have been well cared for and received the attention of both his parents from a young age, but, at the same time, millions of people would not have benefited from the creation of Alibaba.

We all make choices. That's part of life. It is just the way it is. Until we master quantum mechanics, and can be in multiple places at the same time, doing multiple things simultaneously, we are forced to conduct the affairs of a single path, without regrets over the path that could have been.

Choices play a fundamental role in determining the reality that unfolds for us. There are two kinds of choices. The first are the choices you make with both eyes wide open. You know all the alternatives, and you can logically prioritize and decide. The second kind of choice is the type Jack Ma faced—one where you do not see all the alternatives and their consequences as you are moving forward on a singular path with a singular vision.

***

Chapter 8 Understand Your Motivation

"I don't want to be liked. I want to be respected."

Jack Ma

Most people have a goal. However simple and uncomplicated that goal may be, they have a goal. Some want to get a job to pay the rent. Others have a goal to achieve standing in a specific profession. Still others want to have a family and a house in the suburbs. There are many kinds of goals.

Jack Ma had his goals, too. He had a goal when he sent out his college applications, and he certainly had a goal when he went around Hangzhou bartering city tours for English lessons.

But a goal can be a double-edged sword. Goals can be either cause for frustration or the impetus to make progress. It is like driving to the store. If you don't set your goal of going to the store, you will end up driving around aimlessly and burning gas for no discernable benefit.

The difference between someone like Jack Ma and the rest of us isn't whether we have or don't have goals, but is in the kinds of goals we have, the choices we make, and the motivations behind the choice of goals. In many cases, we see a goal and like the idea of it, but we fizzle out, because the motivation to get started and keep going, and the ability to get up after a failure are not there.

That is why you see success stories built on situations where the person had "no choice" but to succeed, because the failure of the endeavor would have brought about such catastrophe that they had to fight hard relentlessly to make it. Having no way out is a great motivator.

Jack Ma was highly motivated. Whether applying for a job as a teenager, or wanting to learn English, his motivation to do the things he had chosen to do was very strong. How do we know what motivation looks like? Instead of trying to describe it, imagine, if you can, the commitment it takes to keep the lights on in a business by taking on a second job. That is what Jack

Ma did when he was supporting Haibo (translation company).

Studying success stories, I discovered that what I had believed important is actually less important. As MBAs (Master of Business Administration), it was drilled into us that startups need to be studied, and business plans needed to take competitor analysis, target markets, and demographics into consideration. It all had to be put into a business plan. Then you had to go out, get funded, and get started. I have tried doing it that way, and you know what always seemed to happen—someone else would beat me to the punch.

Jack Ma did not use market research or competitor analysis. His secret formula was simple—shared prosperity, an inspiration, instinct, and doing everything it took to get it done.

Jack's motivation to get things done was extraordinary. Like many super achievers, Jack was a person who could not rest until he succeeded in achieving his goal. He was relentless about it. But what was different about him from many of the people I have studied is that he did not take shortcuts.

Many could argue that Jack Ma's ideas were shortcuts in that Alibaba was created in the image of Amazon, Taobao was created in the image of eBay, and Alipay was developed in the image of PayPal. But China is a very different market, and Ma's motivations were very different. He did not just copy Amazon, eBay, and PayPal. He looked at the idea of a marketplace and a payment gateway, and he created his own version of it. Saying that he copied Amazon to make Alibaba would be like saying that Elon Musk copied Henry Ford to make a production line for Tesla. Jack Ma openly said, *"Our philosophy is, using internet technology, we can make every company become Amazon."*

It is the process of being motivated that is the key, the reason for the motivation is secondary. You can never define your motivation—it is simply a power you have inside to get done what you are inspired to do. It is like mixing the two parts of an epoxy. There is the resin, and there is the hardener. If you only have the resin, it will not harden; if you just have the hardener but not the resin, the hardened material will be too brittle to be of any use. You need both parts, mixed in precise ratio to get the right result.

Success is similar: you need the two parts of the equation filled precisely; one without the other will not get you anything. The two parts required for any success are the tangible and the intangible.

The inspiration, the intangible, for Jack Ma, was not to become rich (that's not inspiration, that's greed) but was to altruistically redefine the landscape for

Chinese businesses and allow them to trek a path to buyers around the world.

In Jack Ma's case, the tangible part was the active hustle he put into everything he did. If any idea was stuck in his head, he would not rest until he was able to convert that intangible inspiration into a physical manifestation.

The secret to gargantuan success, not just minor achievement, comes from this formula. If you look at history and study the long list of positive successes that men have achieved, and if you took the time to study them intently, you would find that this tangible/intangible duality was satisfied in every single instance.

The inspiration/motivation phenomenon is one that we all understand instinctively but do not really know how to execute. It is the same thing you get when you pray. It is the same thing you get when you conduct rituals. It is even something you do when you wish on a birthday candle and blow it out. Tangible and intangible are two sides of the same coin of success.

Jack Ma instinctively handled those two sides of success by taking tangible action on his intangible inspirations. As a major component of his business, Jack Ma specifically sought after and achieved the intangible asset of trust. He paired that with the manifested physical actions of delivery and guarantee. His response to the fraudulent Gold Star sellers at Alibaba is a perfect example.

Ma's inspiration/motivation matrix is evident in everything he does and in every pairing of tangible/intangible phenomenon that he partakes in. Jack Ma has been motivated to create tangible businesses by intangible things that are literally larger than life and larger than his own needs.

***

Chapter 9 Jack's Four Failures

"Instead of learning from other people's success, learn from their mistakes. Most of the people who fail share common reasons (to fail) whereas success can be attributed to various different kinds of reasons."

Jack Ma

When you study Jack Ma's life, it becomes apparent that he was not flattered by his own strengths, but he was also undaunted by his weaknesses. Like most, Ma made his share of mistakes, but he learnt much about life from them.

Here are five mistakes that contributed to Ma's experience and ultimate success.

1. Failing in school.

Failing at school as many times as Jack Ma would have made it easy to give up. However, we are all given different natural talents and strengths for accomplishing different things.

It is conventional thinking to believe that the academic route is the best way to educate a person, but some of the greatest successes only found academic institutions to be stifling, not liberating. Bill Gates, whom I have also written about, was a school dropout. Mark Zuckerberg was also a dropout. Steve Jobs was another one without academic credentials. All these people were successes because they were revolutionaries.

To be a revolutionary, you cannot think the same old way using the same old methods, you need to reinvent the wheel whenever possible. Conventional schools are not the best way to create unconventional minds.

According to Sir Ken Robinson, education and creativity expert, the fires of creativity are not only not fanned in school, they are positively doused, and the ashes discarded into the bin of mediocrity. Likewise, Jack Ma has begun to argue for changes to education. Ma has been advocating that education should now emphasize creativity, independent thinking, innovation, and imagination, qualities where human beings will always be superior to machines and Artificial Intelligence.

2. Failing at Math.

Jack Ma specifically failed at math. On one test to determine his mathematical competency, Ma got 1 out of 120 possible points. Failure occurred at 70. While Chinese exams are specifically designed to be hard, capable of bringing even the most brilliant of students to their intellectual knees, the only thing Ma's score revealed was that he did not know any of the material covered.

3. Failing to get into Harvard 10 times.

Most people would consider this an example of Ma's tenacity, but I see it as a mistake that could not get past him. Jack Ma applied to Harvard 10 times and was rejected each time. Ma's mistake was thinking that Harvard had something to offer him that he needed.

I encounter scores of people who feel worthless because they don't have a name-brand college degree. Others doubt themselves because they have no degree at all, but that is the worst way to look at one's self. If you cannot see your own self-worth without validating it with a college degree, then you have bigger problems than not having that degree.

Look at the real successes achieved by the giants of history. Although some did go to Ivy League schools, and others went to regular state schools or community colleges, there is a large population of achievers who did not take this conventional route.

So, what was Ma's real mistake? It was trying nine more times to get into Harvard after the first rejection. That was a waste of time. However, Ma was always tenacious about going after what he had set his mind to.

It was a good thing that Harvard had not accepted him. If they had, he might only have gone to work for a billionaire instead of becoming one.

4. Failing to put the right people at the top.

Jack Ma made that known to his initial investors who put in the original $60,000 that they would not be key managers in the running of the company, because he wanted to hire those who were trained and the best in the field. Ma soon learned that was the biggest mistake, because top management who did not have skin in the game were not worth the additional intellectual contribution they brought to the table. When Alibaba was hit with the fraud scandal that shook it to its very foundation, Ma realized that founder's blood was thicker than water. A man who has a personal stake in the rise and fall of the company would do whatever it takes to keep it alive, but an employee can come and go as he or she pleases.

5. Failing to get seed money.

Jack Ma's best "failure" of all was repeatedly failing to get seed capital from Silicon Valley to fund Alibaba. He had turned to Silicon Valley to fund Alibaba during its early stages and was turned down several times. That turned out to be a good thing, although it must have been completely disheartening. His mistake was to waste time with Silicon Valley. There were two different cultures at play, the way Alibaba was run, and the way Silicon Valley expected the companies they invest in to be run. If Ma had gotten that investment, it would have stifled the prospects of the company, and it would not have become the largest IPO in NYSE history.

***

Chapter 10 See the Big Picture

"Trade is a communication of cultures and values."

Jack Ma

Jack Ma gets the big picture. Something in him has been able to see the whole nine yards since he turned 12 and wanted to speak English so badly that he went downtown and offered his services as a tour guide in return for English lessons. It would have been easy for him to offer tours for a dollar here and there, and that would have translated into quite a lot of money. Remember, 15 years later, his entire month's salary was just $12. When he offered tours, he could have made twice that, just in tips, if he had decided to take the money instead. The opportunity cost of learning English from tourists was high, but it was a stroke of genius. Young Jack was able to see the longer term wisdom of learning English.

There was an underlying inspiration that had moved him. This sort of inspiration is actually available to everyone. Whether Jack heard the inspiration consciously or not, he was so strongly driven that he was almost charmed in the actions that he took. Ma obviously understood the bigger picture, and that the picture only grew in dimension and scope, the more successful he became.

Success is not about how rich you get—that is the reward. Success is about how efficiently you make your contribution. Once you make the best contribution you can, the rewards will flow naturally and without interruption. However, if you focus on the rewards, they will usually distract you from successfully making your contribution, and you will ultimately fall short of any achievement worthy of supernatural profits.

Most of the suffering in this world comes from chasing rewards and looking for the least contribution one can make to get the greatest return. That mindset is the best way to get stuck in a rut of mediocrity and to forgo any potential that is within you.

Thus, the question you want to ask yourself should be, "What is my contribution?" That question naturally follows from a sincere desire to make a positive contribution and requires inspiration to answer.

To see the big picture, you cannot be distracted. Most of the time, distractions come by way of rewards and material gain. Most people who chase after the riches end up empty-handed, but those who pursue achievement end up well rewarded.

So, what does it mean to see the big picture?

If you are like Jack Ma, seeing the big picture means looking out for those around you and understanding that we are all just tiles in a larger mosaic. While we are in this mosaic of existence, we are all interconnected, and the one element that connects us is mutual gain and trust.

Without trust, there is a problem with the mutual gain part of the equation. Without mutual gain, there is no equity in the relationship, and that means there is no fairness. Fairness is just another word for balance. When there is no balance, things inevitably seek to return to a state of balance. In some cultures, this is called "karma."

The big picture is all about what you give to society. Typically, the more you give, the greater the reward. It does not matter what you give. As long as it adds value, you have achieved your contribution.

Jack Ma's contribution seems obvious to most people, but, so far, we've looked at what he did in China. But what about the rest of the world? The story of Jack Ma is not only about Alibaba and the group of companies that are involved in trade. Ma is also heavily invested on both sides of the Pacific. In both China and the US, Jack Ma funds a private equity firm, Yunfeng, that invests in up-and-coming companies.

PE (private equity) firms are critical to our economy. Without PE firms, there would not be as many of the companies that are providing significant value to society. PE firms absorb the riskiest phase of a company's development, and provide their understanding of the math behind the endeavor, the quantification of risk. PE firms are experts at this, and Yunfeng has brought their own brand of risk assessment to the industry. Yunfeng assesses the risk/return balance by taking into consideration the people behind the investment, and they bring their risk mitigating strategies and the tools of the Alibaba Group to the table.

Jack Ma uses Yunfeng to advance what he started with Alibaba, which was to make every company into an Amazon and make everyone successful. In Jack Ma's big picture, we are all connected, and we can all achieve mutual benefit and success from a globally connected world.

***

Chapter 11 Saving

"People say, 'Well you know the economy's bad, so China consumption will be low. No, totally different. You Americans love to spend tomorrow's money, and other people's money maybe... We Chinese love to save money."

Jack Ma

During Jack Ma's teaching and translation days, and during the founding of Alibaba, there was a lot of hard work and money was tight for Jack and Zhang Ying. The way they managed to get by, while feeding all those Alibaba people, raising a son, and getting a dream off the ground, was by saving. The Ma household stayed prudent with their budgets and didn't go out to spend lavishly. Saving has been a natural tendency for working-class families in China. It is especially so for those building up a business to take it long term.

Saving isn't something that most North Americans know how to do. In fact, most of us are negative savers. These days, the typical household has more debt than equity and savings, which means that things can turn upside down very fast in the event of an emergency or an unplanned event.

Saving comes naturally to people who aren't looking ahead to the rewards when endeavoring to build a business and contribute. If you were looking to invest with someone, you wouldn't be comfortable investing with a person who had a spending problem. On the other end of the spectrum are those who are thrifty and not prone to high-flying habits, characteristics of those who know how to succeed and are eventually rewarded, like Warren Buffet, Steve Jobs, and Bill Gates.

Those who come from working class families typically learn how to save and conserve from a very young age. Working class families need to stretch their dollar farther. Jack Ma and his wife, also, learned it young, and have continued to apply it in their own family. Although Jack has achieved billionaire status more than three years ago, he still has not gone on a shopping spree. Jack and his wife are simple by nature. They may now be among China's wealthiest people, but that does not mean they dine on caviar and champagne.

Saving is an essential part of contribution. Saving isn't just about the accumulation of resources for later use. Saving is about not draining your resources in the present, and keeping them without the intention of future use. Saving is not about "what ifs." Saving is about putting away most of what comes in and living a life that is simple, without the fat or luxury we are accustomed to seeing some of the rich indulge in.

Saving doesn't just develop good habits. It is also a way to avoid distractions. Becoming wealthy is a function of a mindset that is focused and tuned to a single matter at hand. You cannot have any distractions from the tasks that need to be done to accomplish your end goals. Those tasks need your full attention and concentration. You also need to be aware of all the things going on and noting the effects your actions are having and be able to make real-time adjustments.

Saving, as the successful men of this generation will tell you, is key to becoming successful. You do not save your way to a billion dollars—that takes a lot of pennies—but the habit of saving turns you into someone who keeps costs low and isn't distracted by the pleasures that come from unnecessary spending. It keeps things real. Saving is not about hoarding—saving is about paying attention to the business at hand, rather than to the distractions of spending.

In the early days of Goldman Sachs, Marcus Goldman, the original founder, monitored the books every night as they closed for the day. He was notorious for being absolutely incensed if the books were out of balance even by a penny. It wasn't those pennies that have made the investment bank the titan it is today, but it was the culture and habits of attention to detail, and the laser focus on accuracy that Goldman had instilled in the organization.

Jack Ma's natural ability to live on a tight budget allowed him to focus on big dreams without fantasizing about big expenses and lavish extravagances. It helped him remain on a sure footing as his company took three years to get off the ground; he was able to use some of his own resources to support the operations of the company while it found its legs. The ability to save is not just about keeping money for a rainy day. Many years of true saving allowed the Ma family to endure the years of limited income without feeling depressed and forlorn.

Making money is not about spending it. If you become used to spending the riches you make, it is a sure sign of an impending fall. Jack Ma and his wife continue to keep their expenses in check, and understand the value of frugality and the benefits of cultivating a saving culture.

***

Chapter 12 Infinite Game

"As a business person, I want the world to share the prosperity together."

Jack Ma

In every analysis I do—and you can see this in other books I have written about the titans of the modern world, from Steve Jobs to Richard Branson and Elon Musk—I study men of wide-reaching consequence within a framework that allows me to understand their actions, motivations, and trajectories. In the same way that business analysts use business models, such as Five Force analysis, SWOT, and so on, I use a simple matrix to determine whether individuals are finite or Infinite players.

The key to distinguishing between finite or infinite players is to identify whether they are true to their inherent vibrations, or if they are pursuing goals that will ultimately cause them more distractions. You see, it does not matter whether a person is a finite or infinite player, it only matters that they are well matched to what they are doing. A finite player playing a finite game will be successful. At the same time, an infinite player playing an infinite game will also be successful. The problem arises when a finite player tries to play the infinite game or the infinite player tries to play the finite game. That's when catastrophe awaits.

Finite players are those who are aces at quarterly profits and rapid gains. They make really good CEOs, and they eventually branch out on their own doing exactly what they did for their prior bosses. Finite players hold a special place in society and are a much-needed element in the balance of how we move forward as a species. They provide continuity and they balance the equation with short-term perfection.

Infinite players, on the other hand, are completely different in outlook and vibration. They are in it for the long haul. At times, that infinite player may not appear to be moving forward, but, as in the race between the tortoise and the hare, the infinite player (who is most certainly the tortoise) eventually reaches the finish line to win in the longer term.

Jack Ma, at first glance, has all the earmarks of the finite player. His ideas and Alibaba appear as mirror images of existing companies, seeming to be a perpetuation of more of the same. It could seem that Jack Ma simply knows how to make a good copy of something, but the truth is much more than that. Not everything needs to be reinvented; not everything needs to be patented. When you take a closer look at Ma's motivations, his performance and words, it becomes apparent that Jack Ma is the quintessential infinite player.

Let's consider a comparative example to underscore the differences between finite and infinite players.

When Samsung hit the market with facial recognition software for its phones, Samsung had appeared to beat the more expensive Apple model with a significant leap in technology. Sales soared for the product and the brand. Samsung has consistently been the first to market with technologies that have buoyed their quarterly numbers. On the other hand, Apple, although the leader in the smartphone space, took its time, releasing new technology at an almost Stoic pace. When Samsung rushed out their facial recognition technology, they grew sales, but the technology was soon found to be light on security. The system could be duped using a photograph. When Apple finally released their own facial recognition technology, they had developed it further, using artificial intelligence to map the face. That mapping wasn't limited to mathematical data points on the surface of the face, but also used a thermal map of the face, plus a number of other security features that made it very difficult to overcome.

Like its founder, Steve Jobs, Apple has been an infinite player. Samsung, a finite player, has been driven by quarterlies, stock prices, market share, and whatever is on the next horizon. Apple, on the other hand, has looked beyond the next quarter. Apple waited until their face recognition technology had reached its maturity, instead of trying to be the first one on the block with a new toy. That is the essential infinite player.

Jack Ma is the infinite player. Although he did not go out to make something fresh and new and unproven, he took something that already existed but expanded its uses, enabling a large swath of people to take advantage of it. He found a new use for an existing product. The millions of people who use the site daily cannot distinguish between the person who first created the product and Jack Ma, who brought it to them. Yet, if it was not for Jack, they would not be experiencing the benefits.

Jack Ma's long term, infinite vision of building a platform that would share in prosperity is best illustrated by a true story. During the early stages of setting up Alibaba, when the company was on its way up, revenues were still low, because the benefits were still accruing more to the customer. Jack Ma was still financially strapped. Going to the noodle house for lunch, Ma would be surprised by other business men, who were profiting greatly from the existence of Alibaba, quietly paying for his meal. They would say they knew that, even though they were making money, Ma was not, and paying for his meal was the least they could do.

Infinite players are born, not made, just as finite players are born, not created. The key is being true to yourself and understanding who you are on the finite/infinite plane. If you are an infinite player, play the infinite game, and you will find prosperity. If you are a finite player, play the finite game, and you will find your niche. Do not cross over. That would be a mistake.

Consider the people you read about and whether they are finite or infinite players, and then pay close attention to the ones that most resemble you. So, if you are an infinite player, study the lessons of people like Jack Ma, Steve Jobs, and Elon Musk. If you are a finite player, look to people like Mark Zuckerberg, and Sergei Brin.

***

Conclusion

Jack Ma is an atypical billionaire who made it to the top by looking out for the prosperity of others and understanding the concept of shared prosperity. He realized that the world is not the product of a zero-sum game. Instead, the world is the resulting balance of shared prosperity.

We have seen examples of this at work before. At the end of World War II, the United States knew very well that, without the recovery of Europe, it wouldn't be long before the spiral of economic descent and repercussions from Europe's devastation would reach the United States. To prevent that, the USA adopted the Marshal Plan to help rebuild Europe. The thriving economies of Europe, such as Germany, are the result.

Shared prosperity is the natural flavor of humanity. All of nature lives in balance, and everything in nature progresses only through interaction with each other. If you have no one to sell to, there is no need to build anything. Beggar-thy-neighbor policies never work. But prosper-thy-neighbor policies always do. Jack Ma inherently understood the need to allow everyone to prosper, and that is the foundation of his success.

As a person who wasn't academically inclined or naturally book smart, a lot can be said for the natural talents of Jack Ma, but it wasn't those talents that buoyed him to the top so much as it was his ability to be true to himself. That was what drove him to start and accomplish what he has.

Of course, Ma thought about wealth and riches. The interest in profit is natural. If it were not for profit, there would be no way for him to feed himself or his family, and he would not be able to move forward. Profit is certainly a factor, but the quantity of profit is not the core concern of the typical successful billionaire. When they maintain their primary focus on the contribution they make, as Jack Ma did, their wealth and value builds to exceed all expectations.

One way to look at how to become a billionaire is to not think about being a billionaire. To become a billionaire, instead, think about what you can contribute, what value can you add to the world around you so that it can prosper. How can you enrich the rest of the world? Bill Gates made it possible to have a computer in every home. Elon Musk changed the way we think about energy. Jack Ma made it possible for small and medium businesses to prosper by reaching across oceans and transacting business in a trustworthy way. What is the contribution you can make that you can expand on until it affects the entire world? Find that and you will find your wealth.

Jack Ma is one of the most unexpected billionaires. He does not look the part. No one who knew him in his younger days would ever have expected him to amount to much. He did not have the charm or the looks. He did not have an ivory tower education. He did not have the political or business connections of a wealthy father or a politically connected uncle. He was an everyday kid, growing up in Communist China before it was the industrial powerhouse it is today. I cannot stress enough how ordinary Jack Ma was as a kid, and how ordinary he was as he grew up. He was even too ordinary for colleges and universities, and too ordinary to work at the first KFC that opened in his city.

Now, Jack Ma is the Executive Chairman of Alibaba Group—a company that still holds the NYSE IPO record. Its gross sales volume this year was almost half a trillion dollars, greater than the GDP of Thailand. On Singles Day in China, Alibaba clocked a single day's sales (gross merchandise value) of 17.8 billion dollars. In comparison, Amazon's Prime Day in July clocked in a record-breaking $1 billion over a thirty-hour period. Alibaba sold $1 billion dollars just in the first five minutes of sales on Singles Day.

All that is to show how many lives are touched by Alibaba. And all that was a direct result of Jack Ma being perplexed at being unable to find a single Chinese seller during an online search.

Jack Ma's core value and goal of shared prosperity is the reason he is where he is today. His contribution to the world was not an invention or a gadget. His contribution created real change, making a measurable difference at the kitchen tables of hundreds of thousands of families who became able to reach new customers and generate better incomes for their families. That indeed is a revolution.

If you enjoyed this book, I would be forever grateful if you could leave a review. Reviews are the best way to help your fellow readers find the books worth reading. Thanks in advance!

Make sure to check out the next book in this 'Billionaire Visionaries' series:

Richard Branson: The Force Behind Virgin – Insight and Analysis into the Life and Successes of Sir Richard Branson.

www.ingramcontent.com/pod-product-compliance
Lightning Source LLC
Chambersburg PA
CBHW020618130526
44591CB00042B/239